If You Meet A STRANGER

CAMILLA JESSEL

WALKER BOOKS
LONDON

It's a special day at Olu's playgroup.

ROTHERHAM PUBLIC LIBRARIES

The author gratefully acknowledges the help of the
Save the Children Fund Patmore Project and the
Metropolitan Police Force Community Involvement Unit,
London Borough of Wandsworth.

First published 1990 by Walker Books Ltd
87 Vauxhall Walk
London SE11 5HJ

© Camilla Jessel 1990

Printed by Imago, in Hong Kong

British Library Cataloguing in Publication Data
Jessel, Camilla
If you meet a stranger
1. Children. Interpersonal relationships with strangers
I. Title
302'.024054
ISBN 0-7445-1602-1

Policeman Tony and Policewoman Ann are coming to talk to the children.

They bring two police cars:
WEEEYOOO! WEEEYOOO! WEEEYOOO!

Policewoman Ann teaches the children to say:

"We STOP, and we LOOK and we LISTEN before we cross the road. We must make sure no trucks or cars are near!"

Then the children are given balloons with pictures of zebra crossings on them.

Policeman Tony lets Olu try on his big boots.

Pete tries his huge, heavy jacket.
Paul and Tracy play with the walkie-talkie.

Olu blows Policeman Tony's whistle very loudly:
"WHEEEEEEEE!"

Farida wants to try the handcuffs. "What are handcuffs for, Policeman Tony?"

"To help us catch bad people," says Policeman Tony.

Policeman Tony says, "Now listen carefully."

"Some bad people want to steal things – like cars or watches."

"But some bad people want to take little children away."

"A bad person might tell lies. They might give you sweets or crisps or toys, then make you get in their car."

"So you mustn't EVER, EVER, EVER take ANYTHING from ANYONE without first asking the grown-up looking after you."

Policewoman Ann says, "NEVER GO ANYWHERE with ANYONE without asking the person who's looking after you."

"If anyone wants you to get into their car, or asks you into their house, you shout 'NO!' very loudly."

"Even if someone tries to hold your hand when you don't want to, yell 'NO! NO! NO!' – and tell your mum."

Olu won't forget. She won't go ANYWHERE with ANYONE without asking first.

One day Olu goes to the playground, to play with Paul and his mum.

But why are those two strangers looking at Olu and Paul?

The man and the woman have friendly faces; and they have lollies and crisps.

Olu loves lollies, especially red ones. Paul likes crackly, crunchy, munchy crisps.

Oh dear! Are Paul and Olu going to take the lollies and the crisps?

Or will they remember what Policeman Tony said, that they must never take ANYTHING from ANYONE without asking the grown-up looking after them?
Oh dear! Oh dear! Will they remember?

"Come on, love; have a lolly!" says the man in a soft, kind voice.

Olu says, "NO!"

"Have some lovely, crunchy crisps?" says the lady.

Olu and Paul answer, "NO! NO!"

"Come for a ride in our car: we'll take you to the seaside!"

Olu and Paul say, "NO! NO! NO! We won't go with you. We won't go ANYWHERE with ANYONE without asking first!"

Olu pushes Paul down the slide. "Quick!" she yells.
"Run! Run! Tell your mum!"

She starts to follow Paul, but the woman says, "Your
mum has had an accident. Come in our car. We'll take
you to her, darling."

Olu is frightened, but then she thinks: is that really true?

"You're telling me a lie!" she shouts. "I'm not getting in your car: I'm going to tell Paul's mum!"

She goes whoosh down the slide, and runs very fast after Paul.

She tells Paul's mum what happened.

When they look around, the man and woman have disappeared.

"Clever girl, Olu," says Paul's mum. "Look, they've run away."

They go to the police station.

They want to tell the police about the bad people who tried to get Olu and Paul into their car.

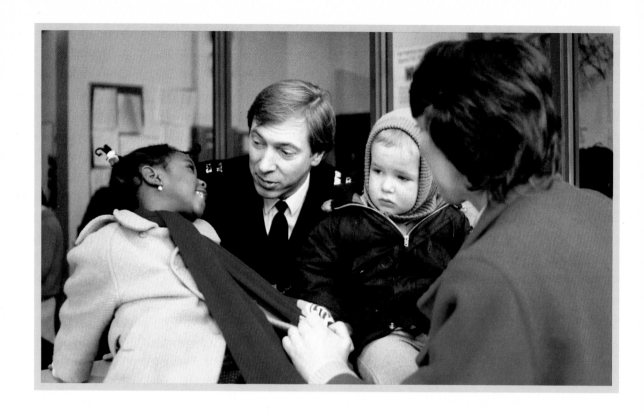

What luck! Policeman Tony is on duty.

Olu says, "We didn't take the sweets or the crisps, and we didn't get into their car!"

"Good children!" says Policeman Tony. "Now, leave it to us; we'll send out a police car to find those people."

"WEEEYOOO! WEEEYOOO! WEEEYOOO!" say Olu and Paul.

"What would you like as prizes for being so clever?" asks Policeman Tony.

"I'd like a ride in your police car," says Paul.

"I want to blow your whistle again!" says Olu.

She blows it very hard.

"OW-OW-OW-OW! OUCH!" says Policeman Tony.